First
Facts®

Transportation Zone

# Airplanes in Action

by Lola M. Schaefer

CAPSTONE PRESS
a capstone imprint

First Facts is published by Capstone Press,
1710 Roe Crest Drive, North Mankato, Minnesota 56003.
www.capstonepub.com

 Books published by Capstone Press are manufactured with paper
containing at least 10 percent post-consumer waste.

*Library of Congress Cataloging-in-Publication Data*
Schaefer, Lola M., 1950–
  Airplanes in action / by Lola M. Schaefer.
    p. cm.—(First facts. Transportation zone.)
  Includes bibliographical references and index.
  Summary: "Describes airplanes, including their history, their parts, how they work,
and how people use them to travel"—Provided by publisher.
  ISBN 978-1-4296-7688-5 (library binding)
  ISBN 978-1-4296-7964-0 (paperback)
  1. Airplanes—Juvenile literature. I. Title. II. Series.
TL547.S3335 2012
629.133'34—dc23                                         2011029161

**Editorial Credits**
Carrie Braulick Sheely, editor; Sarah Bennett and Lori Bye, designers;
    Eric Gohl, media researcher; Kathy McColley, production specialist

**Image Credits**
Capstone Studio/Karon Dubke, 22 (all)
DVIC/Master Sgt. Kevin Gruenwald, 19
Getty Images/MPI, 16
iStockphoto/Sean Locke, 7
Library of Congress, 15
Shutterstock/Carlos E. Santa Maria, 11; Christopher Parypa, 1, 8; devi, 5;
    Pincasso, cover
Wikipedia, 12, 21

Printed in the United States of America in North Mankato, Minnesota.

102011    006405CGS12

# Table of Contents

# Airplanes

An airplane zooms down the **runway** at an **airport**. Whoosh! It rises smoothly off the ground. Inside the plane passengers relax.

Passengers take airplanes to travel long distances quickly. Powerful engines move airplanes through the air.

> **runway:** a strip of level land at an airport that aircraft use for taking off and landing
>
> **airport:** a place where aircraft take off and land

# Flying on a Passenger Plane

Airlines own many large passenger planes. To ride on these planes, passengers buy tickets. At the airport, passengers check in their luggage. They board a plane at an airport gate. Pilots fly the airplane. Flight attendants keep passengers comfortable.

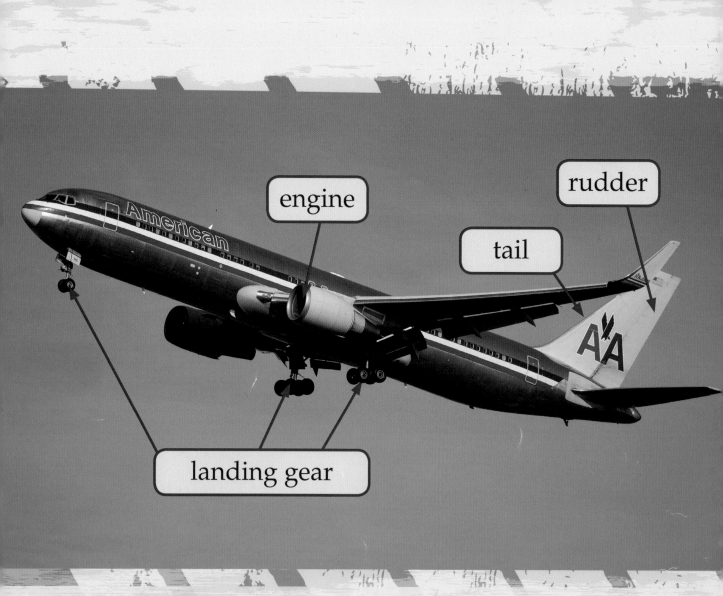

engine

rudder

tail

landing gear

# Parts of an Airplane

Most airplanes have the same main parts. An airplane has a long body with two wings and a tail. Large engines power airplanes.

Pilots use controls in the **cockpit** to fly planes. They move the plane's **rudder** to help steer the plane. They put down the landing gear before landing.

**cockpit:** the place where a pilot sits in a plane

**rudder:** a hinged plate attached to the tail of an airplane that is used for steering

# How an Airplane Flies

An airplane's engines and shape help it fly. Engines on some small planes turn **propellers**. **Jet engines** usually power large planes. These engines push out hot gases. As the gases rush out, the planes move forward.

Airplane wings have a flat bottom and a curved top. This shape helps lift planes into the air.

**propeller:** a set of rotating blades that provides the force to move an aircraft through the air

**jet engine:** an engine that is powered by a stream of gases made by burning fuel and air inside the engine

jet engine

12

# Before the Airplane

Before airplanes, traveling long distances was difficult. Many people made long-distance trips on trains. But trains could travel only where there were tracks. Early cars didn't travel well on rough roads. Ships were the only way to cross oceans. People wanted to make traveling easier, safer, and faster.

# Inventors of the Airplane

Orville and Wilbur Wright were bicycle makers. But they were also interested in flying. The brothers first built **gliders**. In 1903 they invented the first engine-powered airplane. Orville and Wilbur named it the *Wright Flyer*. Orville made the plane's first flight near Kitty Hawk, North Carolina. The plane was in the air for only 12 seconds.

the *Wright Flyer*'s first flight

**glider:** a lightweight aircraft that flies by floating and rising on air currents instead of by engine power

World War I airplanes

# Early Airplanes

Factories began building planes soon after Orville Wright's first flight. Early planes were made of cloth, wood, and wire. Propellers powered these planes. Many early planes were used in World War I (1914–1918).

Over time plane design changed. Builders added seats to old warplanes to make passenger planes. Pilots flew the first jet-engine planes during World War II (1939–1945).

17

## Airplanes around the World

Today people use airplanes to travel around the world. Every day more than 87,000 flights take place over the United States alone. Militaries use planes as weapons and to transport soldiers and gear. Some people have their own small planes. Airplanes are a safe, fast, and dependable way to travel.

# Airplane Facts

- Jet airplanes commonly fly at about 600 miles (965 kilometers) per hour.

- In 1927 Charles Lindbergh became the first person to fly alone across the Atlantic Ocean. His flight took 33.5 hours.

- A Boeing 747 passenger airplane has about 4.5 million parts.

- Most airline passenger planes carry 100 to 250 passengers.

- Large passenger planes can fly 6,000 miles (9,656 km) without refueling.

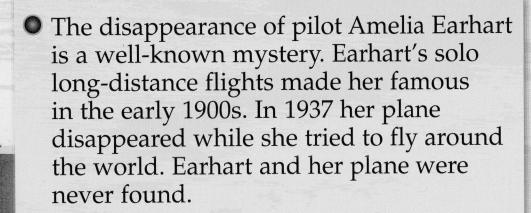

The disappearance of pilot Amelia Earhart is a well-known mystery. Earhart's solo long-distance flights made her famous in the early 1900s. In 1937 her plane disappeared while she tried to fly around the world. Earhart and her plane were never found.

Amelia Earhart

# Hands On: How a Jet Engine Works

Jet engines move airplanes forward with a force called thrust. You can learn how thrust works.

**What You Need**

| | |
|---|---|
| piece of string 10 to 16 feet (3 to 5 meters) long | balloon |
| | tape |
| drinking straw | a friend or other helper |

**What You Do**

1. Tie one end of the string to the back of a chair or a doorknob.
2. Put the other end of the string through the straw.
3. Pull the string tight. Tie it to another chair or doorknob at least 9 feet (3 m) away.
4. Move the straw near one end of the string.
5. Blow up the balloon. Pinch the end of the balloon closed. Place the balloon underneath the straw.
6. Ask a helper to tape the balloon to the straw.
7. Let go of the balloon.

Air coming out of the balloon pushes it forward along the string. The stream of air works like the thrust of a jet engine.

# Glossary

**airline** (AYR-lyn)—a company that owns and flies airplanes

**airport** (AYR-port)—a place where aircraft take off and land

**cockpit** (KOK-pit)—the place where a pilot sits

**glider** (GLYE-dur)—a lightweight aircraft that flies by floating and rising on air currents

**jet engine** (JET EN-juhn)—an engine that is powered by a stream of gases made by burning fuel and air

**luggage** (LUHG-ij)—suitcases and bags people take along when they travel

**propeller** (pruh-PEL-ur)—a set of rotating blades that provides the force to move an aircraft through the air

**rudder** (RUHD-ur)—a metal plate on an airplane's tail that is used for steering

**runway** (RUHN-way)—a long, flat piece of land where a plane takes off or lands

# Read More

**Hubbell, Patricia.** *Airplanes: Soaring! Diving! Turning!* New York: Marshall Cavendish, 2008.

**Miller, Reagan.** *High-Flying Airplanes.* Vehicles on the Move. New York: Crabtree Pub., 2011.

**Spengler, Kremena.** *An Illustrated Timeline of Transportation.* Visual Timelines in History. Mankato, Minn.: Picture Window Books, 2012.

# Internet Sites

FactHound offers a safe, fun way to find Internet sites related to this book. All of the sites on FactHound have been researched by our staff.

Here's all you do:

Visit *www.facthound.com*

Type in this code: 9781429676885

 Check out projects, games and lots more at
**www.capstonekids.com**

# Index